The Civil War
Life Back Home

Nancy-Jo Hereford

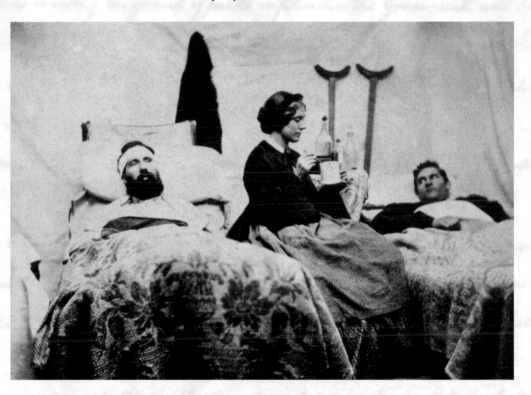

Contents

A Divided Country

When you think of a war, you might imagine soldiers from different countries fighting each other. But wars aren't always fought between countries. Sometimes, groups of people from the same country go to war. This kind of fight is known as a **civil war.**

Nearly 150 years ago, soldiers in our country faced each other in the American Civil War. It took place from 1861 to 1865 and was the bloodiest war in our history. The fight was between two regions—the North and the South.

During the Civil War, Southern and Northern soldiers suffered greatly. The fighting was hard and bloody. Friends became enemies. When it was all over, hundreds of thousands of men were hurt. Many more lost their lives.

During the Civil War, soldiers from the North wore blue uniforms, and soldiers from the South wore gray.

Both sides counted on friends and family left at home. In the North and the South, people on the **home front** provided supplies, such as guns, uniforms, and food.

More than that, the people at home provided hope. They cheered on their troops as they marched off. Loving letters from wives, parents, sisters, and children helped keep up spirits. Many of the younger soldiers had never been away from home before. Knowing their families were thinking of them helped them stay brave during the long years of fighting.

A family in Virginia, in the South

Before the Civil War, some people in the South lived differently than people in the North.

A family in Minnesota, in the North

"*My life here is not very pleasant, but I [give in] to it because I think…it is the duty of us all, to do what we can for our country…. It was given to us entire, and we must give it to you [young people], entire.*"

— An unknown Northern soldier from Rhode Island in a letter to his children, 1861

Reasons for War

Our country went to war with itself because of serious differences between the North and South. Many Southerners made their money from farming. Some of them had large farms known as **plantations.** There, they raised crops such as sugar, rice, and, most of all, cotton.

On plantations, hundreds of workers picked crops from sunup to sundown. Southern farmers needed a lot of help. So, they brought men and women from Africa and forced them to work against their will as slaves. Slaves had no freedom and were paid nothing. If they tried to escape, they were often captured and brought back.

In the North, some people made their money from **industry** instead of farming. Northern factories used machines to make all kinds of goods. Cotton from the South, for instance, was turned into cloth in the North.

These different ways of life made it hard for people of the North and South to understand each other. Many Northerners were against **slavery.** People of the South felt they had the right to run their farms the way they chose.

Workers who were held as slaves look on as a manager measures all the cotton that they picked by hand.

Abraham Lincoln had spoken out against slavery. When he was elected president, Southerners became afraid the government would tell them how to run their plantations.

So, eleven Southern states broke away, or **seceded,** from the country. They named Jefferson Davis as their president and called themselves the **Confederacy.** The Northern states were known as the **Union.** On April 12, 1861, Confederate soldiers attacked Fort Sumter in South Carolina. The Civil War had begun.

The War Between the States

Map Key
- Union states
- Confederate states
- Territories
- ⊛ Capital
- • Other city
- 🏰 Fort

Abraham Lincoln

Jefferson Davis

Four Union states—Maryland, Delaware, Missouri, and Kentucky—decided not to fight and didn't provide soldiers.

Life on the Home Front

People on both sides lost husbands, fathers, and brothers. Many women and older people worked long, hard hours in factories or on farms to produce supplies for the war. Some went hungry as food ran out or was put aside for soldiers. And everyone had to find a way to continue their lives in the middle of war.

The war didn't happen only to adults. Children on the home front suffered, too. During those years, many children had to help their mothers and older sisters take care of their homes. Some children worked in the fields. Others helped the soldiers. Dozens of young boys on both sides brought water and supplies to the fighting men.

The Civil War brought about many changes for children who were slaves and children who were free.

This young soldier was called a "powder monkey" because he brought gunpowder to crews on Union Navy ships.

Kids Write About the War

In the North, Maria Lewis helped her mother run their family farm while her father fought for the Union Army. Maria wrote a letter to her father, telling him how much she missed him.

" ••• *Papa, I will attempt a few lines to let you know that we are all well…. But our minds are never easy…and never will be until your safe return.*"

— Maria Lewis, age 16, Ebensburg, Pennsylvania

Carrie Berry saw a famous battle take place near her home in the South. It was a horrible experience.

"*We have had to stay in the cellar all day; the shells have been falling so thick around the house. Two have fallen in the garden but none of us were hurt.*"

— Carrie Berry, age 10, Atlanta, Georgia

The South at War

When the Civil War started, many people in the South were full of joy. They believed they were fighting for the right to form a new country. But as the war dragged on, year after year, they began to suffer greatly.

Southerners faced many problems that people in the North didn't. For one thing, most of the fighting took place in the South. Soldiers fought in Southern fields, around the plantations, and sometimes right outside of people's homes.

One big battle took place in the city of Fredericksburg, Virginia. Soldiers fought in the streets. Cannonballs fell on houses. Many **citizens** were forced to leave the city to save their lives.

A newspaper from the city of Charleston announced that South Carolina had broken away from the nation in December, 1860.

CHARLESTON

MERCURY

EXTRA:

Passed unanimously at 1.15 o'clock, P.M. December 20th, 1860.

AN ORDINANCE

To dissolve the Union between the State of South Carolina and other States united with her under the compact entitled "The Constitution of the United States of America."

We, the People of the State of South Carolina, in Convention assembled, do declare and ordain, and it is hereby declared and ordained,

That the Ordinance adopted by us in Convention on the twenty-third day of May in the year of our Lord one thousand seven hundred and eighty-eight, whereby the Constitution of the United States of America was ratified, and also, all Acts and parts of Acts of the General Assembly of this State, ratifying amendments of the said Constitution, are hereby repealed; and that the union now subsisting between South Carolina and other States, under the name of "The United States of America," is hereby dissolved.

THE

UNION
IS
DISSOLVED!

When soldiers left their families behind, saying good-bye was hard.

As the fighting drew closer, many families quickly packed up their belongings and left.

One of the leaders of the Union Army was General William T. Sherman. He believed that you could defeat an army by making things tough on the home front. In 1864, his soldiers caused great destruction on a march through the state of Georgia. They burned farms, killed cows and other **livestock,** and ripped up railroad tracks.

General Sherman wanted to make the fight harder for the Confederacy. He wanted to show the South that not only soldiers would suffer if the war continued. The people at home would, too.

Sometimes Union officers completely took over a plantation and set up camp.

"*The* [houses] *that were standing all showed signs of* [an attack], *and on every plantation we saw the* [burned] *remains....*"
— Eliza Andrews, a young girl, after Sherman's soldiers marched through Georgia

The Cost of War

Besides the heavy fighting, people of the South faced serious problems with their **economy.** Many slaves escaped, looking for freedom. This left the plantations without enough workers. For the first time, women and children had to help keep the farms running.

Before the war, there were only a few factories in the South. Crops like cotton were sold to factories in the North. There, factory workers used them to make goods, such as cloth. These goods were then shipped back to the South.

When the war began, President Lincoln ordered a **blockade** of the South. The Union Navy set up ships along the Southern coastline. These ships stopped boats with supplies for the Confederacy.

As the war went on, people in the South had fewer of the things they needed to survive. For instance, there wasn't enough cloth to make new clothing.

Many slaves escaped and joined the Union Army, like these soldiers who also played music to keep up spirits.

Worst of all, food was hard to find. Some people went hungry. When they *could* find food, it was expensive.

Along with working to take care of their families, citizens of the South also worked to give Confederate soldiers the supplies they needed. As the war went on, these things became harder to find, because the Union Navy wouldn't allow any boats to come into the South. The blockade made life difficult for Southerners on and off the battlefield.

The Union Army burned Charleston and other Southern cities, destroying homes and businesses.

Rising Prices

Item	Price in 1861	Price in 1863
Shoes	$25 a pair	$500 a pair
Beef	$1 a pound	$8 a pound
Butter	$3 a pound	$20 a pound
Flour	$8 a barrel	$30 a barrel

This chart shows how prices jumped in the South during the war. The $500 bill of Confederate money that's shown above wouldn't buy you very much!

Women of the South

During the war, most Southern men who were young and in good shape joined the Confederate Army. They left behind their wives, mothers, and sisters. For the first time, women had to take care of the homes, farms, and businesses.

It was a new experience for them. But the women of the South showed they were tough. They worked in the fields and kept track of money and food for their families.

Southern women also helped out as nurses, looking after wounded soldiers. A few worked as spies. They dug up secrets about the Union to help the Confederacy.

Belle Boyd

One of the most famous Confederate spies was named Belle Boyd. It's said that she became a spy at age 17 after Union soldiers broke into her family's home in Virginia. She pretended to be friendly to Union officers to get information. Belle was arrested many times, but didn't give up. Once when she was in jail, she put secret notes inside rubber balls and tossed them to a partner on the street!

Rose Greenhow

Rose Greenhow, who is shown here with her young daughter, was part of high society in Washington, D.C. She threw fancy parties and invited many leaders from the government. While her guests talked business, she eavesdropped. Rose learned many secrets and passed them on to the Confederacy. Eventually, she was caught by the Union police.

Belle Boyd

Rose Greenhow

The North at War

When the war started, many people in the North were angry. They didn't believe the South had the right to the leave the Union. They were willing to fight to keep the United States one **nation.** Northerners cheered as parades of men marched off to become soldiers.

But they weren't cheering for long. It's true that the war made life hard in the South. However, that didn't mean it was an easy war for the North to win. The Union Army lost several important battles during the first two years. Many people believed the Confederate Army had better battle plans.

Winning made the people of the South want to keep going. After a while, people in the North got tired of the war. Their loved ones were away from home. Many Union soldiers were killed or wounded.

Posters like this helped the North find the two million soldiers who signed up for the Union Army.

Back then, letters and photos were the only ways soldiers could stay in touch with the people at home.

President Lincoln knew he needed to give the North a reason to stay in the war. On January 1, 1863, he signed an order called the **Emancipation Proclamation.** It gave freedom to the slaves and made some people in the North want to keep fighting. But freedom would only happen if the Union won. By signing the order, Lincoln changed the Civil War into a fight for a country where all people are free.

When President Lincoln signed the Emancipation Proclamation, it gave the war an important purpose for many people in the North.

"*I started to read the proclamation.... Men* [cried out], *women fainted...white and colored people shook hands, songs were sung.... Men marched...to the White House and congratulated President Lincoln....*"

— Reverend Henry M. Turner, a free African American minister in Washington, D.C., on January 1, 1863

The War Winds Down

Life was not as hard in the North as it was in the South. Northerners had many things that Southerners didn't. Those things made a difference and they helped the Union Army win.

First of all, the North had more people. That meant that there were more men who could be soldiers. In the South, most of the young men went away to fight. In the North, only about half of the men who were old enough to fight were needed as soldiers. The rest stayed home.

This also meant that there were more workers to make the supplies the Army needed. Men working in Northern factories made many guns, cannons, bullets, uniforms, and other goods that kept the war going. Factories also made all the items that people needed to survive. And there were no enemy soldiers burning farms and killing livestock, as in the South.

Only a few battles were fought in the North. So, in many cities, such as New York, life went on as usual.

In the North, some men stayed behind and worked as farmers, fishermen, shopkeepers, and factory workers.

The North had all those things in its favor. What it needed was the right general to lead the Army. About halfway into the war, President Lincoln found that person. With General Ulysses S. Grant in charge, the Union Army finally defeated the Confederate Army in 1865.

At home in the North, people cheered. At home in the South, many cried.

Although some men kept their factory jobs, many women worked there too, making guns and other supplies for the soldiers.

"Our old flag's coming, our brave old flag;
On many a battle field,
It was torn and [ripped] by the shot and shell,
But never would the old flag yield."

— From the Northern song "Coming Home from the Old Camp Ground," 1865

Women of the North

Northern women faced some of the same problems as women in the South. For them, it was also a big change when a husband or father went off to war. They had to take on jobs they hadn't done before, just like Southern women.

Some Northern women helped out as part of the United States Sanitary Commission. This group made sure Union soldiers had food and that their camps were clean.

Several Northern women risked their lives working as spies to dig up Confederate secrets. Others served as nurses, looking after injured soldiers.

Clara Barton

Clara Barton had a hard job. She helped doctors operate on soldiers right near the battlefield. During one operation, cannonballs fell very close by. Some people ran for cover. But Clara stayed put. As the ground shook, she held the operating table steady for the doctor. Clara was called "the Angel of the Battlefield." After the war, she started the American Red Cross to help people in need.

Harriet Tubman

Harriet Tubman was born a slave, but she escaped and ran away to the North. For years, she slipped back into the South on risky missions. Harriet helped hundreds of other slaves run away from their plantations and escape to freedom. During the war, she worked as both a nurse and a spy. Harriet saved many lives, in more ways than one.

Clara Barton

Harriet Tubman

United Again

The Civil War ended with America still one nation. The eleven states of the Confederacy were no longer a "country." They were once again part of the United States. For many people at home in the South, the end of the war meant the end of the life they had known. Their land was a big mess. Everywhere, buildings and bridges were destroyed. Railroad tracks were damaged, too. This meant that Southern soldiers had to walk home. Some walked from Virginia all the way to Georgia and Alabama. That's a long trip to make on foot!

After the war, thousands of Union soldiers returned to the North. This group marched to Washington, D.C.

Families in the North and South welcomed their husbands and fathers home.

Without a doubt, the worst thing for the families in the South was all the husbands, fathers, sons, and brothers who never came home. About 800,000 men fought for the Confederacy. More than 250,000 died. Another 225,000 were wounded. Many men lost arms or legs in battle. So, many women who had run the family farm during the war had to keep on running it after it was over.

But for millions of African Americans, the Civil War had brought about a great change. Lincoln's Emancipation Proclamation had freed all the slaves.

Just as they did during the war, the people of the South showed spirit when it was all over. They rebuilt their homes and cities. Most important of all, they became American citizens again.

Damaged railroad lines made it hard to get fresh supplies into the South after the war.

"*When we heard* [that we were] *free,* [we all] *marched to* [town] *and had a celebration.*"

— Unknown former slave from Alabama

After the War

The people of the North had fought for the "starry banner"—the United States flag. When the war ended, that flag flew again over one country.

The years after the war brought sadness to the North, just as it did to the South. Around two million men fought for the Union. Nearly 360,000 died. More than 275,000 were wounded.

The years after the war also brought many important changes. A law made all former slaves American citizens. For many African Americans, it was the start of new opportunities. Some became **pioneers** in the West. Five years later, African American men also gained the right to vote.

However, women, both white and black, could not vote for the leaders of our country. Even before the Civil War, some women in the North had said that was unfair. They believed this even more when the war was over. Women showed that they were strong during the Civil War. They had done men's jobs on farms and in factories. However, it would take more than 50 years before women could vote. But the Civil War made more women believe they deserved that right.

The years after the war were a big time for industry in the nation. Businessmen built more factories. New railroads moved people and goods to growing cities in the West.

The country was filled with new energy. The war was over and so was the long fight over slavery. Now the people of the United States were eager to make a bigger and better America than ever before.

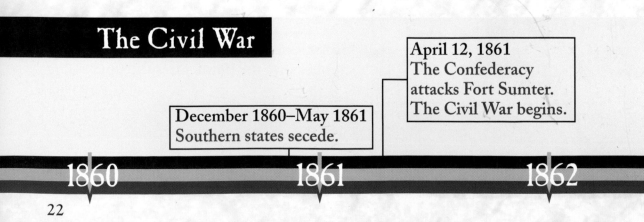

The Civil War

December 1860–May 1861
Southern states secede.

April 12, 1861
The Confederacy attacks Fort Sumter.
The Civil War begins.

1860   1861   1862

At a celebration almost fifty years after the war, these two army **veterans** proudly shook hands. One fought for the North and the other for the South.

This statue in Washington, D.C., honors the African American soldiers who served during the war.

Many lives were lost on both sides during the Civil War.

January 1, 1863
Lincoln issues the Emancipation Proclamation.

November 15–
December 21, 1864
General Sherman's March to the Sea destroys Southern property on the home front.

April–May, 1865
The Civil War ends.

1864   1865   1866

Glossary

blockade a line of ships that blocks a port or harbor to keep boats from entering or exiting

citizen a person born in a country or who chooses to become a member of that country by law

civil war a war between citizens of the same country

Confederacy the eleven Southern states that broke away from the United States in 1860–1861

economy the ways a community makes and uses its money and resources

Emancipation Proclamation the order issued by President Abraham Lincoln on January 1, 1863, that ended slavery in the United States

home front the place where citizens live while soldiers are at war

industry a group of businesses that makes one kind of product

livestock the animals raised as a source of income for farmers or ranchers

nation a country or a community of people that comes together under a single government

pioneer a person who moves to an unsettled area to begin a new life

plantation a large farm that usually grows one kind of crop

secede break away or leave

slavery the system of keeping people as slaves. Slaves have no freedom and are forced to work without receiving pay.

Union the group of states that remained part of the United States after the Southern states seceded in 1860–61. Most Union states were located in the North.

veteran a person who once served as a soldier